# The Companion Guide to
# Part One of *Nurturing Love*

# The Companion Guide to Part One of *Nurturing Love*

Salima Sanford

Mistletoe Press

Design by Meadowlark Publishing Services.

Cover and interior illustrations by Patty Schork Wear.

Author photo courtesy of the author.

Published by Mistletoe Press.

nurturing99@gmail.com

Manufactured in the United States of America.

ISBN 979-8-9855111-3-0
Published 2025

# Contents

# Introduction

*Nurturing Love* was written over several years, a sharing of insights emerging from the trials and blessings of my marriage. Each discovery was tested and fine-tuned until woven into the fabric of our relationship. Each level of understanding opened into a deeper space for new insights to emerge.

The tools and concepts described in *Nurturing Love* become useful through practice, so I developed this companion book as a participatory guide. When read in parallel with *Nurturing Love*, each chapter of this guidebook invites you to engage in activities that augment the original teachings and to note your experiences, with the goal that together, the two books will better meet your needs. You may use the spaces provided here to respond to the writing prompts—workbook style—or dedicate a separate journal or notebook for this purpose. This companion book also lends itself to being read and worked with in a group setting, for a rich sharing of experiences and insights.

Lasting change in a relationship does not occur overnight. This guide presents an opportunity to slow down your consideration of the book's concepts, make them more intimate, and allow time for self-reflection and spiritual connection. You will be invited to unearth your opinions and judgments, beliefs and attachments, emotions and needs, in search of the essential truths within you.

It is my hope that this guide will become a helpful companion as you chart your own path to find, fill, and overflow with the unconditional nurturing love of which we all are capable. If that is your desire, then welcome, and may your journey be blessed.

—Salima Maryam Linda

# 1

## Toward Loving-Kindness

## Focus: Exploring love

*Whoever misses love, misses everything because love is the secret of life. This is why people must be aware and be careful not to break hearts ... because this is not a game ... Love is from God and this is why it was actualized and realized in the hearts of the lovers. It is a very holy thing.... Be a soft earth. Be an easy land, expansive and full of love.*

Love is everywhere and always. Love knows no boundaries. We taste love, or mourn its seeming absence, so often, in so many ways and depths over our lifetime.

Let our exploration begin.

## An Honest Look

Recall a recent memory that was positive for you, an event, sight, taste, sound, or interaction about which you might you say, "*I loved that.*" It may be as simple as a special meal or as powerful as an interaction with nature or with a loved one.

What did you love about that memory?

_____

_____

_____

You may use the Feelings and Needs chart in the appendix to identify what feeling(s), need(s), and/or inner qualities this memory of love evoked in you.

_____

_____

_____

Suppose you could never have this particular experience again. Can you imagine another experience that would fulfill this same need?

_____

_____

_____

And now, for balance, name two things you currently do *not* love—behaviors, tastes, events, or other experiences.

1. _____

_____

2. _____

_____

For each of the two events or situations that you do not love, consider what feelings and needs that are of importance to you seem diminished or not satisfied.

Situation 1: feelings aroused and/or needs not met.

_____

_____

Situation 2: feelings aroused and/or needs not met.

_____

_____

# Going Deeper

### Three Aspects You Love

Bring your spouse to mind. *Identify three aspects you love about him.* These may be behaviors, qualities, or routines you see in him every day, or very rare observations you don't often see but you know are there. Please take ample time for your answers. In your thoughts and observations, something new or forgotten may come to mind.

With regard to the three aspects you love in your husband, what feeling and need does each one satisfy in you?

1. I love

_____

This quality makes me feel

_____

and satisfies my need(s) for

_____

2. I love

_____

This quality makes me feel

_____

and satisfies my need(s) for

_____

3. I love

_____

This quality makes me feel

_____

and satisfies my need(s) for

_____

## *One Characteristic You Are Not Fond Of*

Now name one characteristic you see in your spouse that you are *not* fond of at this time in your life. For example, what trait or pattern of behavior do you seem to have the most difficulty with?

I am not fond of

_____

This characteristic makes me feel

_____

and does not meet my need for

_____

### *Qualities You Carry*

*To walk the path of love means to start on the journey to yourself.*

Now identify one or two qualities *you* carry that you feel are helpful in your relationship with your husband and/or in other close relationships.

_____

_____

In review, select one answer for each statement below.

What I appreciate most in my spouse is

_____

What I am having trouble accepting in my spouse is

_____

Now let's look at pairing some of your responses regarding the qualities you see in yourself and your husband.

First, consider a quality or characteristic your husband does not often provide for you (in your estimation). Then identify a quality you carry that balances this seeming lack. For example, let's say your husband is quick to anger, while you are patient.

His quality or characteristic that you are not fond of:

_____

Your quality or characteristic that mitigates this quality:

_____

Briefly describe how your trait compensates in the marriage for his seeming shortcoming.

_____

Secondly, consider one of the qualities you stated you liked best about your husband placed alongside a quality that is not your strength.

His lovable quality or characteristic:

_____

A quality or characteristic of yours that is softened by his quality:

_____

Comment on how his trait balances an area of weakness: e.g., his equanimity balancing your impatience.

_____

_____

Over time we learn from the strengths of the other and more clearly see the wisdom in our match, the possibility of nourishing a wholeness in the sacred union of marriage. Our goal should not be the absence of struggle but rather to find in the fire of the challenges the majesty of strengthening love—for ourselves and our marriage.

## Practices and Pledges

Sometimes we do not really see our partners, or we see them through the eyes of judgment. We may see them with our minds but not with our hearts. There are instances where we may even, unawares, avoid noticing them because of behaviors that currently put us off.

### *Quietly Notice*

Here is a useful exercise to help you begin to see your husband through new eyes. Start to notice your spouse unawares when he is occupied in doing something. From a place of love and curiosity, imagine what lies beneath the activity for him; what about it gives him pleasure, or irritation; or even what just creates changes in his body. While going unnoticed yourself, observe his spirit more closely in expectation of a surprise or something new to be found.

When you see something in your husband's nature you have not noticed before, and when it feels right, allow yourself to show appreciation for this deeper understanding, through touch or kindness. You need not verbally share your discovery. You are seeing through new eyes something private, something possibly not even within his awareness. Your satisfaction will be the pleasure of your discovery and the resurgence of love in your heart for this newfound mystery of his being

Record your observation:

_____

_____

Finally, each day notice some facet of *yourself* that you may feel good about and/or that you wish to send compassion to. Make a note of this below, lest you forget this tender look at your being.

_____

_____

May you continue to:

> . . . *open your heart … and allow the water of the ocean of the love to flow within so that you may live in the stations of the divine beauty.*

# 2

# Laying the Foundation

## Focus: Relationship expectations

Complaining, as Mullah Nusruddin does in chapter 2 of *Nurturing Love*, is acceptable as a means of venting and a source of relief and comfort for the lover. Even masters of patience and perseverance complain to God, the only Source of all that is needed.

Acknowledging our difficulties, bringing them into the light, aids our understanding, our tolerance, and our ability to embrace all that marriage brings, for *Even as (love) ascends to your height and caresses your tenderest branches that quiver in the sun, So shall he descend to your roots and shake them in their clinging to the earth.*

## An Honest Look

It is natural to want to complain, at times, about something your spouse does that irritates you. Facing your objections actually opens the door to new ways of responding that leave more space for love to enter.

Take a moment to consider what currently bothers you most about your husband, a behavior that at this period in your life you are having trouble accepting.

Short description:

_____

_____

_____

When you witness this behavior, what assumptions do you make about him? For example, *Anyone who does that must be ...*

Jot down your current assumptions.

_____

_____

_____

## Going Deeper

As children we received information about love from the opinions and behaviors of the adults in charge, and thus, based on our history, we acquired opinions and behaviors regarding the giving and receiving of love that we may now find unhelpful.

Take another look at the behavior of your husband's that you identified.

Is it a behavior you were never allowed to express and and/or one you now work hard not to express?

Is it a behavior that reminds you of a childhood threat to your safety, peace, comfort, or autonomy?

We all share challenges on the path to love, and getting to know our history with love can be helpful. The above questions give examples of experiences that may limit the breadth and depth of our capacity to give and receive love—a never-ending walking.

Reflecting upon your early experiences with loving and being loved, and having mercy for yourself, describe what you now think is a main source of your objection to your husband's behavior pattern.

_____

_____

_____

Now imagine a situation in which your husband manifests the behavior that challenges you, and, remembering that we are all holy beings, take a moment to *send him mercy* from your heart, abandoning your objections and inviting yourself to see this pattern of behavior in a new light, without comment or judgement. (Some strategies for moving from judgement to compassion can be found in Appendix 2.)

What did sending mercy look like, feel like? Did it take the form of words? If so, what words came to mind? Was it a feeling without words? Where in your body did you experience this feeling?

_____

_____

_____

# Practices and Pledges

*Only the loving find love.*
—D. H. Lawrence

*It is very important for love to be actualized, not by words, but by actions.*

*If God is to come, the ego must go.*

Objection to a behavior often entrenches it, whereas love can change any heart. For the next five days, or more, witness this particular behavior of your husband's without judgment. This may require great effort on your part, but it is a necessary and heartwarming part of nurturing love. Your efforts will be a gift for you both.

In the first chapter you were invited to look more closely and more kindly at one another. Now you have been invited to focus on a behavior of your spouse that you find objectionable, to investigate the source of your discomfort, and to find the mercy for you both.

When you have completed this five-day exercise, describe the results of the effort you have made:

_____

_____

_____

*Be in expectation of receiving God's generosity.*

Copy the following revised paragraph from *Nurturing Love* (page 20) to remind you that love begets love.

*The truth is that as I practice love, my love for my spouse will grow deeper. The more I love him, the more love will flow through me from the infinite Source, and the more love I will eventually receive. My husband may not always love me in the way I would have asked for, or ever imagined, but I will recognize it as love as I come to know his heart from which it blossomed.*

_____

_____

_____

_____

_____

# 3

# Commitment to Your Marriage

## Focus: Renewal of your vows

## Inspiration

*Marriage is a very sacred covenant. It is a contract that reflects a covenant between you and God; it is not, "I love you today, but tomorrow I will not love you in the same way." Marriage is a walking toward God, if a person knows how to walk through the marriage … to reach the station of the unity and the oneness.*

## An Honest Look

*Meditation:* Find a comfortable space where you can allow yourself some uninterrupted time alone. Once you have settled in, begin to imagine a benevolent unseen presence embracing and supporting you and your marriage. Welcome this support, from God, angels, or even the spirit of an ancestor whom you felt carried for you great love and wisdom. Take your time. Let your experience of being held in a divine presence fill the room. Your desire is to tap into a vast and ever-present loving support for you, your husband, and your union. Allow this experience to expand and anchor in and around your being.

How does it feel to you? Soft? Comforting? Loving? Expansive? Wise? Strong? Joyful?

Allow this spiritual presence to surround and hold you, your husband, and the union between you. Stay in this place for long enough to create an experience to which you can return again and again, especially when you feel frustrated and alone.

From this experience of being held, you will now be invited to look at your marriage.

Reflect upon the early history of your marriage, how you came into each other's lives, and how fate may have seemed to intervene to keep you together. As you reflect upon the ebb and flow of your relationship, recall a memory of some lucky event that seemed to renew your commitment to love.

If you cannot identify one of the scenarios below, then recall any memory of a positive turning point in your marriage.

Was there a serendipitous event without which you might not have dated or even met your spouse?

Was there a time you might have separated but for a fortuitous turn of events?

Perhaps just when you were feeling that being married was too difficult, you had an epiphany, or heard or witnessed something profound, and that light of understanding enabled you to see your spouse through new and more loving eyes.

Or maybe you simply remember something your husband does that always elicits a surge of love in you.

Record below your personal positive event that supported your marriage.

_____

_____

_____

## Going Deeper

Quite frequently, when we let go of control of how we want our relationship to be, what follows is even better than we could have imagined.

Bring to mind a pattern in your relationship for which you would like to rewrite the habitual script of interaction—for both of you. Perhaps you are certain you'd be much happier if your husband could just change his part in this predictable script. In fact, you probably have already told him how you would like him to change, but without success. Through the exercise that follows, to the extent that you are able, you are invited to drop your attachment to this imagined improvement, as well as to any methods of control you may wish to exert to make it come about.

Find a quiet space and take some time to sympathetically feel your own disappointments and imperfections. After compassionately sitting with your heart, take a similar look at your husband, holding his weaknesses and imperfections tenderly.

Feel your heart opening in relief. Feel the release of the desire to be in control, in the certainty that you alone know what is best. Open your heart to peace and mercy for your two imperfect beings. Allow your body and spirit to rest in expectation of the renewal of your love.

The truth is that _love is all both you and your husband seek,_ though your pictures of love may be different for each of you, especially when you are feeling disconnected from one another.

## Practices and Pledges

Your challenge for the next week is to take some time each day to consciously let go of _ought to_ and _should_ in relation to your husband, and begin to imagine his support and love for you, which is abiding, if you but look deeper. As your compassion for both of you increases, over time you may even begin to find humor in each of your foibles.

Record your experience:

_____

_____

_____

*How do we purify and clean our love? With love; by growing love and by caring for that love until it becomes like a tree, bringing forth fruit and flowers, and by preserving this holy relationship and holy being, and preserving this divine beauty that manifests through the husband and the wife and through the human species. This is why it is necessary for any two lovers who are together and who want this love to continue to renew their divine covenant with each other so their relationship can grow and the love between them can grow and be blessed until they achieve what God meant from them and for them and they follow the straight path.*

For both you and your husband, behind this marriage union lies the light of truth, love, contentment, and self-knowledge and an experience of a holy, abiding intimacy between you. If your decision is to stay in your marriage, certain that your union is a blessed gift, then renew aloud your devotion to this marriage.

Speak aloud, for yourself, your pledge, a statement of your commitment, a renewal of your vows, until your words convey the clarity and beauty you desire. Record that vow below.

_____

_____

_____

_____

# 4

# Our Hidden Treasure

## Focus: Embracing your inner gifts

*The divine light is you, O human being. You think of yourself as a tiny
microcosm, but you carry the whole macrocosm … Every one of us must
preserve and guard what we carry within ourselves … this divine mirror
and light. Only then can happiness be achieved and only then can love,
mercy, justice, peace, and freedom be actualized and become true.*

*The human is holy because we are created from the light of God.*

## An Honest Look

> *When you live in the outside world you are a mirage, but inside this*
> *mirage there is a treasure. Open this treasure to find the jewels inside.*
> —Paraphrased from *Music of the Soul*

With every step on the path to healing, we come closer to who we really are, to that truth within. Our real self is a holy being; we all carry the same potential. Let your light shine forth. Everyone benefits, and contentment will be yours. Imagine yourself through God's eyes. The only judgement you will encounter will be your own.

The way we see ourselves is extremely important. It guides how we move in the world. At times we may wobble along the spectrum between feelings of arrogance and worthlessness, but our true self sits midway, seeing the perfection of every moment regardless of how it appears. Even our mistakes serve our growth.

It is said that to be generous, we must be rich, so let's address some divine qualities that might easily fill your cup to overflowing.

What is the nature of the light you carry?

Allow yourself to take a good look at some of the qualities, gifts, or ways of being that you most appreciate in yourself, and that others appreciate in you.

Underline any of the following words that come to mind when you consider what you most appreciate in yourself, and/or add your own:

> *compassionate, helpful, peaceful, protective, strong, kind, wise, capable,*
> *loving, forgiving, a good friend, trustworthy, good listener, generous,*
> *steadfast, thankful, appreciative, subtle, supportive, flexible, patient,*
> *honest, positive, fun, graceful …*

Now complete this sentence:

I am grateful that God has given me the gift(s) of …

_____

Select the one or two qualities you most identify with at the present moment. Then complete this sentence that follows and read it aloud:

This I know to be true—I am:

_____


Consider the last time you felt the beauty and pleasure of carrying one of these qualities or gifts, whether you were alone or interacting with others, and briefly describe the situation below.

_____

_____

_____


## Going Deeper

Now that you have brought to light one or two qualities you identify with and cherish, let's explore what you feel may hinder your natural expression of them.

For example, you may be peaceful by nature but feel that your husband's anger hampers your natural expression of peacefulness. Or you yourself may be limiting the expression of your peaceful nature. For example, some form of inner wounding—which we all experience—may contribute to a loss of confidence, anger, or other feelings that override your peaceful nature.

While no one is at fault for these constraints on our better nature, the circumstances we find ourselves in and the choices we make can dim our light; yet in our discomfort lie the seeds for exploration and growth.

Select one quality you value and want to embrace and then describe something that might be limiting its full expression.

The quality:

_____

The impediments to its shining forth:

_____

_____

_____


## Practices and Pledges

### Celebrate Your Inner Beauty

For the next week, focus on a quality you carry that makes you feel good about yourself. Each day notice experiences that *reveal and enhance* that part of your nature. Make a note of your experiences, even if the occasion feels small. The goal is to own and grow this part of your nature, for the benefit of yourself and others. In addition, as you pay closer attention to this gift, you may also begin to notice qualities in yourself that bring pleasure to you and others. Observe how you begin to recognize these same qualities being mirrored back to you by others.

Record your experience below.

_____

_____

_____


We begin to see how loving ourselves expands our love for others, and loving others increases our love for ourselves.

### Prayer

I invite you to make frequent simple prayers of gratitude throughout the day over the upcoming week. Notice how your love begins to expand as a result—for yourself, your companions, creation, and Creator, as well as for life's hindrances, for they too are your teachers.

*Live the richness and kindness of your true being: acquire knowledge,*
*do good, be kind to all living beings and thus attain your peace and your*
*inner dignity.*

# 5

## A Subtle Shift

## Focus: There is only One

*All your needs can be met in the container of service to God. You can love God in your spouse and love God through your spouse. You can serve God by tending to your husband in a manner that pleases God. You are merely returning love to its Source through the man whom God has ordained for you to be with, for life.*
—Paraphrased from *Nourishing Love*, page 50

# An Honest Look

## *Shifting Our Perspective*

In previous chapters you have taken a closer look at yourself, your husband, and your marriage. You have avowed your commitment to your marriage, knowing that this decision is in the highest good. Hopefully you now feel the certainty that God put you two together in spite of, or perhaps because of, your differences.

This chapter encourages you to make a subtle but critical shift in the way you relate to your husband. This change in perspective will be particularly useful if you feel stressed about having to divide your time between your spouse and your spiritual work, or if your spouse describes himself as a nonbeliever and regularly objects that your spiritual interests take you away from him.

Marriage is a holy union; the union of you both is much greater than the sum of your parts. The truth is that your relationship is only and always about love, which knows no limits.

What helped me arrive at this understanding was a change in perception and actions. Rather than seeing my husband as existing apart from my spiritual interests, I related instead to a fellow human carrying identical qualities, with the same access to love, forgiveness, wisdom, and so forth as all humanity. It was as if I spoke not to him but to this place of our shared divinity. It wasn't hard, and it has made all the difference. There is no separation when one sees only the Oneness. And then, unsurprisingly, I saw the beauty and integrity that he had always carried but that I had not *seen*.

As a result, what I did and what I said to him were determined less by his reactions than by my guidance as to what felt right and good. When I related to him from this new place, I felt an inner warmth and appreciation that made me feel like a *good person*. To feel your own goodness is a precious thing, and my kindness was rewarded with that feeling.

The other shift was that there was no longer separation between the parts of my daily life. Now there was a unity, a wholeness. I was loving God through my husband and was loving my husband in a manner pleasing to God. There was, as all the holy books say, only One.

# Going Deeper

Keeping in mind the possibility of enhancing your feeling of Oneness and love, I offer this suggestion for your growth:

## *Shifting Your Attention*

For the next five days, withhold all words of negative reaction to your husband, whether spoken or expressed through facial and bodily movements. Withhold all outward manifestations of criticism, correction, displeasure, judgment, aversion, or distaste for any of his behaviors (unless they are extreme). This includes behaviors as small as not shutting the pantry door (do it yourself) or as continually frustrating as his being grumpy, critical of you, not listening to you, and so on.

Avoidance is not a solution and is not the idea here. Instead see, hear, and feel the behaviors you currently have a low tolerance for, but let those behaviors pass without commentary from you. If he is short-tempered, tend to your own needs, with minimal judgement on your part. If he goes too far (which he may later recognize but not admit to), then take some time to remove yourself from his presence and nourish yourself with music, prayer, time in nature, or whatever else suffices. Share with him where you are going, and as you leave him, give him a reassuring kiss or touch.

When a certain behavior continues to be difficult for you to tolerate—for example, impoliteness, short-temperedness, or walling off—use this time of frustration to go inward and hold yourself in love. Invite a greater understanding of why certain behaviors are unacceptable to you but not to him.

There are no quick solutions, but it behooves you to make an effort in two ways. One is to investigate your own reaction and its underlying history, and the other is to develop an understanding of what drives your husband's behavior so as to develop compassion for him. Remember that it may be easy to misinterpret his intent, and intention is a critical consideration.

Your husband may not yet be able to see his behavior through your eyes, particularly when you outwardly object to the behavior. Intolerance aids and abets the continuance of disliked behaviors, while love, tolerance, and understanding will, over time, lead to a diminishing of the behavior. It is miraculous what unconditional love can do.

You have the capacity to take on this challenge. Now find the willingness.

When you have finished this practice, write down some of your thoughts about the experience.

_____

_____

_____

## Practices and Pledges

> *See your partner as a mystery.*
> *Let your love be new to you in each moment*
> *and your relationship will rarely feel stagnance.*
> —Andrea Gibson, poet

### *Feelings of Gratitude, Tenderness, Admiration, Love, or Joy*

Now let's try another practice. For each of the next five days, notice something your husband commonly does, however small, that feels really good to you. Maybe you have previously overlooked this behavior or taken it for granted. Observe this behavior anew, and *express* your gratitude through touch, attentiveness, joy, or words or deeds of appreciation. Your pleasure is not so much for what he did but for who he is.

Record daily each deed and your reaction. Then, at the end of this five-day exercise, you are invited to share any overall changes in your feelings toward your husband: for example, greater fondness, appreciation, patience, or love.

Day 1:

Event _____

Response _____

Day 2:

    Event_____

    Respose_____


Day 3:

    Event _____

    Response _____

Day 4:

    Event _____

    Response _____


Day 5:

    Event _____

    Response _____


Next, note any overall shift in your heart toward your husband:

_____

_____

_____

### *An Invitation to Pray*

Whether you are in the midst of or have completed the two activities in this chapter, taking time for prayer will be beneficial. Ask for what you need—be it comfort, strength, guidance, or something else—and trust that help will come in unexpected ways.

Seek your own way to best find connection in prayer. Prayers of thanks are always beneficial, but so is taking time for honest conversation with your Lord. It is not as if you have any secrets from God, so give yourself the gift of conversing with God for long enough that your deepest needs, thoughts, and feelings can surface.

If a particular prayer has moved your heart, record it below. It may be sweet to look back upon it at a later date.

_____

_____

_____

# Appendix 1

## Center for Nonviolent Communication Charts: Feelings and Needs

Grateful acknowledgment is made to The Center for Nonviolent Communication for permission to reprint these charts.

### Feelings When Needs Are Satisfied

**Affectionate**
compassionate
friendly
loving
open-hearted
sympathetic
tender
warm

**Engaged**
absorbed
alert
curious
engrossed
enchanted
entranced
fascinated

interested
intrigued
involved
spellbound
stimulated

**Hopeful**
expectant
encouraged
optimistic

**Confident**
empowered
open
proud
safe
secure

*Excited*
amazed
animated
ardent
aroused
astonished
dazzled
eager
energetic
enthusiastic
giddy
invigorated
lively
passionate
surprised
vibrant

*Grateful*
appreciative
moved
thankful
touched

*Inspired*
amazed
awed
wonder

*Joyful*
amused
delighted
glad
happy
jubilant
pleased
tickled

*Exhilarated*
blissful
ecstatic
elated
enthralled
exuberant
radiant
rapturous
thrilled

*Peaceful*
calm
clear-headed
comfortable
centered
content
equanimous
fulfilled
mellow
quiet
relaxed
relieved
satisfied
serene
still
tranquil
trusting

*Refreshed*
enlivened
rejuvenated
renewed
rested
restored
revived

# Feelings When Needs Are Not Satisfied

*Afraid*

apprehensive
dread
foreboding
frightened
mistrustful
panicked
petrified
scared
suspicious
terrified
wary
worried

*Annoyed*

aggravated
dismayed
disgruntled
displeased
exasperated
frustrated
impatient
irritated
irked

*Angry*

enraged
furious
incensed
indignant
irate
livid
outraged
resentful

*Vulnerable*

fragile
guarded
helpless
insecure
leery
reserved
sensitive
shaky

*Aversion*

animosity
appalled
contempt
disgusted
dislike
hate
horrified
hostile
repulsed

*Confused*

ambivalent
baffled
bewildered
dazed
hesitant
lost
mystified
perplexed
puzzled
torn

### Disconnected

alienated
aloof
apathetic
bored
cold
detached
distant
distracted
indifferent
numb
removed
uninterested
withdrawn

### Yearning

envious
jealous
longing
nostalgic
pining
wistful

### Disquiet

agitated
alarmed
discombobulated
disconcerted
disturbed
perturbed
rattled
restless

shocked
startled
surprised
troubled
turbulent
turmoil
uncomfortable
uneasy
unnerved
unsettled
upset

### Embarrassed

ashamed
chagrined
flustered
guilty
mortified
self-conscious

### Fatigue

beat
burnt out
depleted
exhausted
lethargic
listless
sleepy
tired
weary
worn out

*Pain*
agony
anguished
bereaved
devastated
grief
heartbroken
hurt
lonely
miserable
regretful
remorseful

*Sad*
depressed
dejected
despair
despondent
disappointed
discouraged
disheartened
forlorn

gloomy
heavy-hearted
hopeless
melancholy
unhappy
wretched

*Tense*
anxious
cranky
distressed
distraught
edgy
fidgety
frazzled
irritable
jittery
nervous
overwhelmed
restless
stressed out

# Needs Inventory

*Physical Wellbeing*
air
food
movement/exercise
rest/sleep
sexual expression
safety
shelter
touch
water

*Honesty*
authenticity
integrity
presence

## Connection

acceptance
affection
appreciation
belonging
cooperation
communication
closeness
community
companionship
compassion
consideration
consistency
empathy
inclusion
intimacy
love
mutuality
nurturing
respect/self-respect
safety
security
stability
support
to know and be known
to see and be seen
to understand and
    be understood
trust
warmth

## Play

joy
humor

## Peace

beauty
communion
ease
equality
harmony
inspiration
order

## Autonomy

choice
freedom
independence
space
spontaneity

## Meaning

awareness
celebration of life challenge
clarity
competence
consciousness
contribution
creativity
discovery
efficacy
effectiveness
growth
hope
learning
mourning
participation
purpose
self-expression
stimulation
to matter
understanding

# Appendix 2

## Moving from Judgment
## to Compassion*

Following are some aids for moving from separation to connection, following discord and judgment:

- Distinguish between the person and their actions.
- See the event without interpretation, as if through a video camera.
- Imagine yourself in their shoes, with empathy.
- Ask yourself what you need in this moment to get back to love
- Satisfy this need through meditation or prayer.
- Release any anger or resentment.
- Drop the need to be right.
- Find a place of peace inside.
- Admit your own contributions.
- Reconnect to the love you have for this person.
- Be in forgiveness for you both.
- Speak and listen from your heart, when ready.

Remember: the love that brought you together still resides in your hearts.

---

\* Adapted by the author from a University of Sufism Level-3 Advanced Spiritual Peacemaking class.

# Notes

1. Be an easy land, expansive and full of love: Muhammad al-Jamal ar-Rifa'i, *The Secret of the Love of God*.

5. To walk the path of love means to start on the journey to yourself: Rosina-Fawzia Al-Rawi, *Divine Names: The 99 Healing Names of the One Love* (Northampton, MA: Olive Branch Press, 2015), 183.

7. so that you may live in the stations of the divine beauty: Muhammad al-Jamal ar-Rifa'i, *The Secret of the Love of God*.

9. So shall he descend to your roots and shake them in their clinging to the earth: Kahlil Gibran, *The Prophet* (New York: Knopf, 1923), 11.

11. It is very important for love to be actualized, not by words, but by actions: Muhammad al-Jamal ar-Rifa'i, *The Secret of the Love of God*, 43.

11. If God is to come, the ego must go: Al-Rawi, *Divine Names*, 183.

12. Be in expectation of receiving God's generosity: Sidi Shaykh Muhammad Sa'id al-Jamal ar-Rifa'i ash-Shadhuli, *The Meaning of the Names of Our Lord* (Pope Valley, CA: Shadhiliyya Sufi Center, 2001) 29.

13. walk through the marriage … to reach the station of the unity and the oneness: Muhammad al-Jamal ar-Rifa'i, *The Secret of the Love of God*, 70.

16. until they achieve what God meant from them and for them and they follow the straight path: Muhammad al-Jamal ar-Rifa'i, *The Secret of the Love of God*, 73.

17. Only then can love, mercy, justice, peace, and freedom be actualized and become true: Muhammad al-Jamal ar-Rifa'i, *The Secret of the Love of God*, 16.

17. The human is holy because we are created from the light of God: Muhammad al-Jamal ar-Rifa'i, *The Secret of the Love of God*, 38.

18. Open this treasure to find the jewels inside: Sidi Shaykh Muhammad Sa'id al-Jamal ar-Rifa'i ash-Shadhuli, *Music of the Soul: Sufi Teachings* (Petaluma, CA: Shad`hiliyya Sufi Center, 1994), 173.

20. be kind to all living beings and thus attain your peace and your inner dignity: Al-Rawi, *Divine Names*, 248.

# Bibliography

Al-Rawi, Rosina-Fawzia. *Divine Names: The 99 Healing Names of the One Love.* Northampton, MA: Olive Branch Press, 2015.

Ar-Rifa'i, Muhammad al-Jamal. *The Secret of the Love of God.* Sidi Muhammad Press, 2006.

Ar-Rifa'i ash-Shadhuli, Sidi Shaykh Muhammad Sa'id al-Jamal. *The Meaning of the Names of Our Lord.* Pope Valley, CA: Shadhiliyya Sufi Center, 2001.

Ar-Rifa'i ash-Shadhuli, Sidi Shaykh Muhammad Sa'id al-Jamal. *Music of the Soul: Sufi Teachings.* Petaluma, CA: Shadhiliyya Sufi Center, 1994.

Gibran, Kahlil. *The Prophet.* New York: Knopf, 1923.

# About the Author

Salima Linda holds a Masters of Divinity degree from the University of Spiritual Healing and Sufism (2009). She is a respected Muqqadim Murabbi in her Shadhdhuliyyah Sufi community, and through her teachings and healings, is connected to people of faith in many parts of the world.

Currently a core teacher at the Institute of Spiritual Healing, she is also a certified Master Healer, a graduate of Dr. Ibrahim Jaffe's training. Utilizing the experience gained in her decade of practice she is able to help others move through the doorway of each challenge into greater peace, love, understanding, and connection to God.

Salima is also the author of *Healing Your Marriage by Healing Yourself* and is devoted to the topic of peace in marriage. Her Sufi name is derived from the quality Salaam, meaning peace, safety, and wholeness. Salim is often translated as "river of peace," a quality she naturally carries.

www.ingramcontent.com/pod-product-compliance
Lightning Source LLC
Chambersburg PA
CBHW081540120626
46550CB00009B/2811